PUFFIN BOOKS

A RIOT OF RIDDLES

What comes once in a minute, twice in a moment, but not once in a thousand years?

The letter M

Here's a collection of over two hundred riddles guaranteed to give you hours of fun, entertainment and . . . torture!

The first chapter introduces you to different sorts of riddles and will give you clues as to how to solve them. Then you're on your own! But don't worry, if you're really stuck the answers *are* at the back of the book.

There are classic riddles, mystery riddles, animal riddles, letter riddles, D–I–Y riddles, silly riddles and even fool a friend riddles to really catch your best friend out.

So have a go, and see whether you can amaze your family and friends by becoming a riddling genius.

Gyles Brandreth has had a busy and varied career. He's had more than fifty books published on a whole range of topics. He's also written television scripts and is a well-known television personality. Gyles is owner of the Teddy Bear Museum in Stratford-upon-Avon, founder of the National Scrabble Championships, creator of the British Crazy Golf Open and one-time European Monopoly Champion!

Other books by Gyles Brandreth

THE DO-IT-YOURSELF GENIUS KIT
THE EMERGENCY JOKE KIT
JOKE BOX
WORD BOX

For younger readers

THE GHOST AT NO. 13
THE HICCUPS AT NO. 13
THE MERMAID AT NO. 13

A
Riot of
Riddles

Gyles Brandreth

Illustrated by
Judy Brown

PUFFIN BOOKS

PUFFIN BOOKS

Published by the Penguin Group
Penguin Books Ltd, 27 Wrights Lane, London w8 5TZ, England
Viking Penguin, a division of Penguin Books USA Inc.
375 Hudson Street, New York, New York 10014, USA
Penguin Books Australia Ltd, Ringwood, Victoria, Australia
Penguin Books Canada Ltd, 2801 John Street, Markham, Ontario, Canada L3R 1B4
Penguin Books (NZ) Ltd, 182–190 Wairau Road, Auckland 10, New Zealand

Penguin Books Ltd, Registered Offices: Harmondsworth, Middlesex, England

First published 1991
10 9 8 7 6 5 4 3 2 1

Text copyright © Gyles Brandreth, 1991
Illustrations copyright © Judy Brown, 1991
All rights reserved

The moral right of the author and illustrator has been asserted

Printed in England by Clays Ltd, St Ives plc
Filmset in Bembo

CONTENTS

WHAT'S IN A RIDDLE?

When first I appear I seem mysterious,
But when I am explained I am nothing serious.
What am I?

A riddle, of course.

What is a riddle? It is more than a joke. It is a
kind of puzzle where in the question there should
be just enough clues to lead you to the answer.

Riddles have been around for a very long time.
The famous Riddle of the Sphinx, from ancient
Greece, is a good example. The Sphinx was a
horrible monster with the face of a woman, the
body of a lion and the wings of a bird. Everyone
who passed her by was asked this riddle, and if
they could not answer it, they were killed:

> What is it that goes on four legs in the
>   morning,
> Two legs at noon,
> And three legs in the evening?

To save your life, can you unravel the riddle?

The answer is: *a human being*. In the morning of our lives, when we're babies, we crawl on all fours. In the middle of our lives we walk on two legs. In the evening of our lives we use a walking stick, giving us three legs.

The great Greek writer, Homer, who lived three thousand years ago, had a lot of trouble with *this* riddle. It was put to him by some fishermen he met on the island of Ios:

> What we caught we threw away;
> what we didn't catch we kept.

The answer is a horrid one. In fact the answer is a lousy one because it's *lice*! If you have ever had lice in your hair you'll know the riddle works: the ones you catch you throw away, the ones you can't catch you keep.

Not so long ago – in fact, only one thousand three hundred years ago – a monk called Bede conjured up some crafty riddles:

> Tell me, what is it that fills the sky and the whole earth, tears up new shoots and shakes all foundations, but cannot be seen by eyes or touched by hands?

The answer is: *the wind*.

The answer to *this* one isn't nearly so obvious:

I am sitting above a horse which was not born, whose mother I hold in my hand. What am I?

The answer is: *a horse drawn by a pen*. Bede is sitting at his desk, looking at a drawing of a horse. He is above the horse. Because the horse is only a drawing it was never born. It was created by a pen — its mother — which Bede is holding in his hand.

Another monk who loved riddles was Dr Claretus who lived in Bohemia six hundred years ago. He produced terrible teasers like these:

> Like grass it is green, but it is not grass,
> Like blood it is red, but it is not blood.
> It is round and smooth like an egg.
> What is it?

The answer is: *an apple*.

This next one isn't easy, but it's very clever:

> A vessel have I
> That is round as a pear,
> Moist in the middle,
> Surrounded with hair;
> And often it happens
> That water flows there.

The answer is: *an eye*.

(Dr Claretus also invented a rather rude riddle:

> What did the world hear?
> *The horse when it farted in Noah's ark*.)

Over the years, lots of riddles have been written as rhymes. Lewis Carroll, who wrote *Alice's Adventures in Wonderland*, loved rhyming riddles. Here's one he invented in 1870:

> Three sisters at breakfast were feeding the
>   cat.
> The first gave it sole – Puss was grateful for
>   that.
> The next gave it salmon – which Puss
>   thought a treat.
> The third gave it herring – which Puss
>   wouldn't eat.
> Can you explain the cat's behaviour?

Lewis Carroll even put the answer into rhyme:

That salmon and sole Puss should think very grand
Is no such remarkable thing.
For more of these dainties Puss took up her stand;
But when the third sister stretched out her fair hand,
Pray why should Puss swallow her ring?

J. R. R. Tolkein, who wrote *The Hobbit* and *The Lord of the Rings*, is another famous English writer who loved rhyming riddles:

> What has roots as nobody sees,
> Is taller than the trees,
> Up, up it goes,
> And yet never grows?

The answer: *a mountain*.

> It cannot be seen, cannot be felt,
> Cannot be heard, cannot be smelt.
> It lies behind stars and under hills,
> And empty holes it fills.
> It comes first and follows after.
> Ends life, kills laughter.
> > What is it?

Darkness.

> A box without hinges, key, or lid.
> Yet golden treasure inside is hid.
> > What is it?

An egg.

With some riddles there is more than one answer. If I said to you:

What's black and white and red all over?

you might say:

A newspaper,
Or *a sunburnt zebra,*
Or *an embarrassed penguin,*
Or *a skunk with nappy rash,*
Or even *a chocolate sundae with tomato ketchup all over it.*

There are at least three possible answers to *this* famous riddle:

What goes over the water
And under the water,
But doesn't touch the water?

The answer could be simply *a ray of sunshine.* Or it could be *a duck's egg inside the mother duck.* Or – wait for it! – it could be *a person crossing a bridge carrying a pail of water on their head.*

Some riddles are simple:

What is easy to get into but hard to get out of?

Trouble.

Some are not so simple:

I sat and I ate and from me one ate,
And below me one ate and above me one
ate.
How could this be?

A woman is sitting on a horse beneath a cherry tree feeding her baby. She eats, the baby eats, a bird in the tree eats and the horse grazes.

As soon as you know the answer to a riddle, the answer seems obvious. For example, the nursery rhyme about Humpty Dumpty is really a riddle:

Humpty Dumpty sat on a wall,
Humpty Dumpty had a great fall,
All the king's horses and all the king's men
Couldn't put Humpty together again.

Because you know Humpty Dumpty is an egg, the riddle seems very easy. Here's another old nursery riddle that won't seem so easy unless you already know the answer:

Hitty Pitty within the wall
Hitty Pitty without the wall
If you touch Hitty Pitty
Hitty Pitty will bite you.
Who or what is Hitty Pitty?

Hitty Pitty is a stinging nettle!

In this book, you will find 250 riddles of all shapes and sizes waiting to sting you. If you get stuck, the answers begin on page 88.

Have fun!

1 CLASSIC RIDDLES

Let's begin with some more riddles that have been around for hundreds of years. When you get used to the old-fashioned way they are worded, you will find they are not as tricky as they at first appear. Good luck!

1   It has cities, but no houses;
    It has forests, but no trees;
    It has rivers, but no fish.
            What is it?

2   As I was going over London Bridge,
    I saw something in the hedge.
    It had four fingers and one thumb,
    And was neither fish, flesh, fowl nor
        bone.
            What was it?

3 Something was here since the
     world was
   First made, and just a month old.
         What's that?

4 Long neck and no hands,
   Hundred legs and can't stand,
   Runs through the house of a morning,
   Stands behind the door when company
     comes.
            What is it?

5 What has eyes but never sees?
   What has a tongue but never talks?
   What has a soul that can't be saved?

6 I tremble at each breath of air,
   And yet can heaviest burdens bear.
            What am I?

7 What is it that a mother loves very
     dearly,
   But which can never welcome her
       when she comes home?

8 There is a thing that when it has a root,
   It has no leaves;
   And when it pulls up its root,
   The leaves appear.
            What is it?

9   A red maiden is sitting in a green
summer-house,
If you squeeze her she will cry
And her tears they are as red as blood,
But yet her heart is made of stone.
What is she?

10   As I was going to Worcester,
I met a man from Gloucester.
I asked him where he was going
And he told me to Gloucester
To buy something that had neither top
nor bottom,
But which could hold flesh, blood, and
bones.
What is it?

11   Ten men's strength, and ten men's
length,
And ten men cannot set it on end;
Yet one man can carry it.
What is it?

12   There is a kind of a tree
Which you can cut down today
And tomorrow it will begin to sprout
again.
What is it?

13 The man who made it did not want it;
The man who bought it did not use it;
The man who used it did not know it.
What was it?

(This is riddle number thirteen, so the answer could be unlucky.)

14 A messenger that could not speak, bearing a letter that was not written, came to a city that had no foundations.
Who was the messenger?
What was the letter?
Where was the city?

(You will find the answer in the Bible as well as on page 88.)

15 The air alone gives birth to this.
It lives without a body.
It hears without ears.
It speaks without a mouth
What is it?

16 Them has got eyes ain't got no head,
An' what got head ain't got eyes.
What are they?

2 MAKING A SPLASH!

These riddles are wet, wet, wet!

17 What gets wetter the more it dries?

18 What is round as a dishpan, deep as a
tub,
and still the oceans couldn't fill it up?

19 Three girls stood under an umbrella but
none of them got wet.
How was that?

20 What holds water yet is full of holes?

21 What is it that never freezes?

22 Crooked as a rainbow,
Slick as a plate,
Ten thousand horses
Can't pull it straight.

23 What has four eyes and cannot see?

24 When will a net hold water?

25 What often falls but never gets hurt?

26 There were five men walking along and it started to rain. The four that ran got wet and the one that stood still stayed dry.

How come?

27 A man went for a walk.
It started to rain.
The man didn't have a hat.
He wasn't carrying an umbrella.
He kept on walking.
His clothes got wet.
His shoes got wet.
But his hair didn't get wet.
How come?

3 WHAT AM I?

28   I am taken from a mine, and shut up in
a wooden case, from which I am never
released, and yet I am used by almost
everybody.

What am I?

29   East, west, north, south,
I've a hundred teeth but never a mouth.
What am I?

30   Use me well and I am everybody;
Scratch my back and I am nobody.
What am I?

31   Twenty of me will fit in a box,
But one of me will fill a barn.
What am I?

32 I carry the heaviest loads and yet I have no back. Men and beasts from far and wide tramp over me and I always stay in the same place.

What am I?

33 I have a little house which I live in all
  alone,
Without doors, without windows,
And if I want to go out I have to
  break through the wall.

What am I?

34 I am a poor iron knight,
I have no arms but always point right.
I have no feet but I must always go
And must stand on duty both day and
  night through.
If ever I rest, all will complain.

What am I?

35 My fatherland is Arabia,
Though in England they roast me
  brown.
I'm ground up inside a mill
And tortured with scalding water
And then they pour milk over me
And drink me at their leisure.
  What am I?

36 You can take away my first letter,
And my second letter.
You can take away all my letters,
And yet I remain the same.
  What am I?

4 FAMILY MATTERS

Think carefully here. With these puzzling riddles it's very easy to jump to the wrong conclusion!

37 There were two Brazilians walking down the road. One Brazilian was the father of the other Brazilian's son.
How are they related?

38 A boy's grandfather is only five years older than the boy's father.
How come?

39 Is it possible for a man to marry his widow's sister?

40 Your uncle's sister is not your aunt.
     Who is she?

41 A man is looking at a photograph of a member of his family. He says: 'Brothers and sisters have I none but that man's father is my father's son.'
     Who is in the photograph?

42 Why is a room full of married couples empty?

43 If a girl falls into a well, why can't her brother help her out?

44 A father was driving his daughter to school when their car was hit by an oncoming lorry. The father wasn't hurt, but the daughter was injured and was raced to hospital by ambulance. She was wheeled into the operating theatre. The surgeon took one look at her and said: 'I can't operate on this child. She's my daughter!'
     Why not?

5 SURPRISE YOUR EYES

You can't believe everything you see, as you will discover with these surprising picture riddles.

45 Is the hat taller or wider?

46 Which line is longer, the top one or the bottom one?

47 How many of these lines are curved?

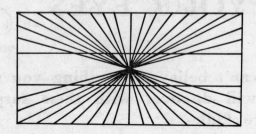

48 Which of the two shaded circles is bigger, the one on the left or the one on the right?

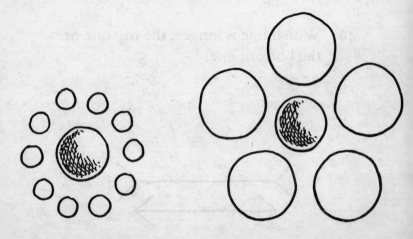

49 Is this a rabbit or a duck?

50 Is the shaded side of the box inside or outside?

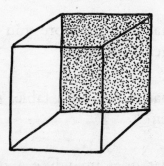

6 WHAT? *WHAT?* WHAT?

51 What runs round the garden without moving?

52 What belongs to you, but others use it more than you do?

53 What is it the more you take away the larger it becomes?

54 What is put on a table, cut, but never eaten?

55 What goes up white and comes down yellow?

56 What is always coming but never arrives?

57 What hangs on the wall without nail or string?

58 What is too much for one, enough for two, but nothing at all for three?

59 What person helps to bring up hundreds of people?

60 What invention allows you to see through walls?

61 What happened when the man sat on a pin?

62 What was the highest mountain before Mount Everest was discovered?

63 What can pass before the sun without making a shadow?

64 What has teeth but cannot eat?

65 What has four legs and one back but can't walk?

66 What has only two backbones but a thousand ribs?

67 What has a neck but no head?

68 What has a face but no mouth?

69 What has a tongue but no mouth?

70 What comes once in a minute, twice in a moment, but not once in a thousand years?

71 What have feet and legs and nothing else?

72 What is it has four legs, one head and a foot?

73 What is it that you can keep after giving it to someone else?

74 What question can never be answered by 'Yes'?

75 What is it that you will break even as you name it?

76 What is big at the bottom, little at the top, and has ears?

7 FOOD FOR THOUGHT

These riddles are good enough to eat.

77 As I went over Padstow Bridge
Upon a cloudy day,
I met a fellow, clothed in yellow;
I took him up and sucked his blood,
And threw his skin away.
    Who was he?

78 The sun cooked it, the hand broke it off,
The foot trod on it and the mouth
    enjoyed it.
        What was it?

79 There was a green house.
Inside the green house there was a
white house.
Inside the white house there was a red
house.
Inside the red house there were a lot
of little black beetles.
You are looking for fruit.
Which one?

80 In marble walls as white as milk,
Lined with a skin as soft as silk;
Within a fountain crystal clear,
A golden apple doth appear.
No doors there are to this stronghold
Yet thieves break in and steal the gold.
You are not looking for a fruit
this time, so what is it?

81 What goes over the fields all day, and
sits in the cupboard all night?

82 With what vegetables do you throw
away the outside, cook the inside, eat
the outside, and throw away the inside?

Here are two riddles, with just one answer:

83 It stands on its one leg with its heart in its head.

> What is it?

84 Patch upon patch without any stitches,
Riddle me that and I'll buy you a pair
of breeches.

> What is it?

85 What kind of ear cannot hear?

86 A farmer had eggs for breakfast every morning. He owned no chickens and didn't get eggs from anybody else.

> Where did he get the eggs?

87 What two things can't you have for breakfast?

88 If it takes three and a half minutes to boil an egg, how long does it take to boil four eggs?

8 WORDS, WORDS, WORDS

89 What eight-letter word has one letter in it?

90 What two words have thousands of letters in them?

91 When is it correct to say 'I is'?

92 Where does Thursday come before Wednesday?

93 Luke had it first.
Paul had it last.
Boys never have it.
Girls have it but once.
Miss Jolly had it twice in the same place, but when she married Peter Jones, she never had it again.

What is it?

94 There is a word in the English language, the first two letters of which signify a male, the first three a female, the first four a great man and the whole a great woman.

What is it?

95 What word of three syllables contains twenty-six letters?

96 What part of London is in France?

Each line in these two rhyming riddles will lead you to a different letter of the alphabet. Put the letters together and you will find the answer.

97   My first is in south but not in north,
My second is in picture but not in film,
My third is in fourth and also in worth,
My fourth is in book and also in cook,
My fifth is in toe but not in sew,
My sixth is in life but not in death.
My whole is a place you *all* must go!

98   My first is in apple and also in pear,
My second is in desperate and also in dare,
My third is in sparrow and also in lark,
My fourth is in cashier and also in clerk,
My fifth is in seven and also in ten,
My whole is a blessing indeed unto men.

9 MYSTERY RIDDLES

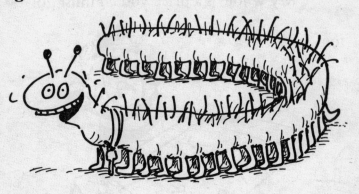

You might expect Riddle Number 99 to be this old favourite:

What goes ninety-nine bonk?

Yes, that's right: *a centipede with a wooden leg.*

That's what you might expect, but *A Riot of Riddles* is full of the unexpected, which is why Riddle Number 99 is going to be the first of our Mystery Riddles, riddles that are like mini detective stories. What you have to do is read each case history very carefully and then decide what really happened.

99 THE CASE OF TOM, DICK, HARRY AND LARRY

Tom, Dick, Harry and Larry all lived together in the same house. One night Tom and Dick went out for a meal. When they got back at about midnight they were horrified to find Larry lying dead in a pool of water on the floor. They knew that Harry was the murderer, but they didn't tell the police.

How come?

100 THE CASE OF THE ONE-WAY STREET

A policeman saw a lorry driver going the wrong way down a one-way street, but didn't stop him.

Why not?

101 THE CASE OF THE WANDERING BEAR

Once upon a time there was a bear that decided to go for a walk. It walked one mile south. Then it turned and walked one mile east. Then it turned again and walked one mile north. It ended up exactly where it had begun.

What colour was the bear?

102 THE CASE OF THE TWO BUTCHERS

There were two butchers standing behind the counter in a shop. One butcher is short and the other is tall. The tall butcher is the father of the short butcher, but the short butcher is not the son of the tall butcher.

How are they related?

103 THE CASE OF THE SAD MAN

With a heavy heart a sad man pushed his car up to a hotel. He was sad because he knew he had lost all his money.
What was going on?

104 THE CASE OF THE RISING TIDE

You are on board your private yacht moored off the coast of the Costa Packet in the Atlantic. Hanging over the side of the yacht is a ladder with twelve rungs. The distance between each rung is 50 centimetres and the lowest rung is just touching the surface of the water. The tide is coming in and the water is rising at the rate of 10 centimetres an hour. How soon will the surface of the water cover the sixth rung from the top of the ladder?

105 THE CASE OF THE WEATHER FORE-CASTER

The weather forecaster woke up in the middle of the night and, much to his surprise, found that it was pouring with rain. He hadn't expected it to rain that night because it was summertime. However, now he had seen the rain, he predicted that in 72 hours time there would still be no sign of sunny weather. How could he be so sure?

106 THE CASE OF THE SILENT PARROT

Polly Kettle decided to buy herself a talking parrot as a pet. She went to the pet shop where the assistant showed her a beautiful bird and told her: 'I guarantee that this parrot will repeat every word it hears.' Polly bought the parrot and took it home where she quickly discovered that the parrot would not and could not speak a single word. What was strange was that the pet shop assistant had only told Polly the truth. Can you explain the mystery?

10 RHYMING RIDDLES

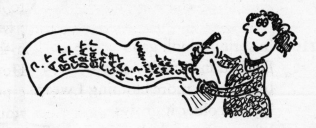

In days gone by, all the best riddles were written in rhyme. It made them easier to remember, even if it didn't make them easier to solve.

107 Little Nancy Etticoat
In a white petticoat
And a red nose;
The longer she stands
The shorter she grows.
What is she?

108 Riddle me, riddle me, riddle me ree,
I saw a nutcracker up in a tree.
What was it?

109   Long legs, crooked toes,
       Glassy eyes, snotty nose.
            What is it?

110   In spring I look gay
       Decked in comely array,
       In summer more clothing I wear;
       When colder it grows
       I fling off my clothes,
       And in winter quite naked appear.
            What am I?

111   What is it that has a tongue but never
         talks,
       Has no legs but always walks?

112   Runs smoother than any rhyme,
       Loves to fall but cannot climb.
            What is it?

113   Pray tell me, friends, if you can,
       Who is that highly favoured man,
       Who though he's married many a wife,
       May yet be single all his life?

114   Goes to the door and doesn't knock,
Goes to the window and doesn't rap,
Goes to the fire and doesn't warm,
Goes upstairs and does no harm.
        What is it?

115   A riddle, a riddle, as I suppose;
A hundred eyes and never a nose.
        What is it?

116   Riddle me, riddle me, what is that
Over the head and under the hat?

117   What's in the church, but not the
       steeple,
The parson has it, but not the people?

118   Never sings a melody, never has a song,
But it goes on humming all day long.
        What is it?

119   Thirty white horses upon a red hill,
Now they champ, now they clamp,
And now they stand still.
What are they?

11 RIDDLES WITH A DIFFERENCE

Here's a different kind of riddle.

What is the difference between a greedy person and an electric toaster?

Shall I tell you?

One takes the most and the other makes the toast.

Here's another one.

What is the difference between a boy going upstairs and a boy looking upstairs?

Can you work it out?

One is stepping up the stairs, while the other is staring up the steps.

Here's a much more difficult one.

What is the difference between a pussy cat and an English sentence?

One has claws at the end of its paws, the other has a pause at the end of its clause.

Now you've got the idea, have a go at these.

120   What is the difference between a door-mat and a bottle of medicine?

121   What is the difference between a jeweller and a jailer?

122   What is the difference between a hungry man and a greedy man?

123   What is the difference between a crazy rabbit and a counterfeit coin?

124   What's the difference between Noah's ark and Joan of Arc?

125 What's the difference between 100 and 1,000?

The next two riddles are to do with dogs and they are a little bit different as well.

126 What is the difference between a man and a running dog?

127 What is the difference between a dog and a flea?

This is a riddle and a joke all mixed up. Try it on a friend. You start by asking the question.

What is the difference between a thunderstorm, a lion with toothache and a pot of glue?
I don't know.
The thunderstorm pours with rain and the lion with toothache roars with pain.
What about the little pot of glue?
That's where you get stuck.

12 ANIMAL CRACKERS

128 If a daddy bull eats three bales of hay and a baby bull eats one bale, how much hay will a mummy bull eat?

129 What kind of bird is always around when there's something to eat or drink?

130 What has a head like a cat, feet like a cat, tail like a cat, but is not a cat?

131 What has six legs, but only walks with four?

132 What makes a lot of noise
In a house with one door,
And if it sits in a draught,
You can't hear it no more?

133 What has four legs like an elephant, a trunk like an elephant, looks just like an elephant, but is not an elephant?

134 Who spends the day at the window, goes to the table for meals and hides at night?

135 Who flays himself, does not die from it, and walks without feet?

136 How was it that a dog tied to a 12-foot rope, managed to walk 30 feet?

137 What is lesser than a mouse,
And hath more windows than a house?

138 Riddlum, riddlum, raddy,
All head and no body.
　　　　What is it?

139 What goes to sleep
with its shoes on?

140 On the way to a water hole a zebra met six giraffes. Each giraffe had three monkeys hanging from its neck. Each monkey had two birds on its tail. How many animals were going to the water hole?

141 What small chest is full of mouse bones?

142 My back as frying-pan does appear;
     Beneath a snowy breast;
     A pair of scissors jut in the rear;
          What am I? Have you guessed?

143 Why are playing-cards like wolves?

144 I'm out and about all day and yet I always
     stay at home.
                    What am I?

145 I'm called by the name of a man,
     Yet am as little as a mouse;
     When winter comes I love to be
     With my red target near the house.
                    What am I?

146 Why are ducks sad?

147 If three birds are sitting on a fence and
     you shoot and kill one of them, how
     many will be left?

13 FOOL A FRIEND!

Let's take a break from serious riddling and have some fun. Here are nine trick riddles for you to try out on your friends.

YOU: Ask me if I'm a cat.

YOUR FRIEND: *Are you a cat?*

YOU: Yes. Now ask me if I'm a dog.

YOUR FRIEND: *Are you a dog?*

YOU: No, stupid. I just told you I'm a cat!

YOU: Would you hit somebody after they had surrendered?

YOUR FRIEND: *No.*

Now you can hit your friend and announce: 'I surrender!'

YOU: How do you keep a fool in sus-pense?

YOUR FRIEND: *I don't know. How do you keep a fool in suspense?*

YOU: I'll tell you next week.

YOU: Look at that henweigh in the garden!

YOUR FRIEND: *What's a henweigh?*

YOU: About 3 pounds.

YOU: I bet I can make you say black.

YOUR FRIEND: *I bet you can't.*

YOU: What's the colour of the Union Jack?

YOUR FRIEND: *Red, white and blue.*

YOU: See, I told you I could make you say blue.

YOUR FRIEND: *No, you said I'd say black.*

YOU: You just did.

YOU: You'd better keep your eyes open tomorrow.

YOUR FRIEND: *Why?*

YOU: You'll bump into something if you don't.

YOU: What is red and goes ding-a-ling?

YOUR FRIEND: *A red ding-a-ling.*

YOU: What is green and goes ding-a-ling?

YOUR FRIEND: *A green ding-a-ling.*

YOU: What is yellow and goes ding-a-ling?

YOUR FRIEND: *A yellow ding-a-ling.*

YOU: What is orange and goes ding-a-ling?

YOUR FRIEND: *An orange ding-a-ling.*

YOU: No, you're wrong. They don't make them in that colour.

YOU: What has six legs and barks at strangers?

YOUR FRIEND: *I don't know.*

YOU: A dog.

YOUR FRIEND: *A dog?*

YOU: I gave it two extra legs to make it harder.

YOU: Will you remember me in fifty years?

YOUR FRIEND: *Yes.*

YOU: Will you remember me in twenty years?

YOUR FRIEND: *Yes.*

YOU: Will you remember me in ten years?

YOUR FRIEND: *Yes.*

YOU: Will you remember me in five years?

YOUR FRIEND: *Yes.*

YOU: Will you remember me next year?

YOUR FRIEND: *Yes.*

YOU:	Will you remember me next month?
YOUR FRIEND:	*Yes.*
YOU:	Will you remember me next week?
YOUR FRIEND:	*Yes.*
YOU:	Will you remember me tomorrow?
YOUR FRIEND:	*Yes.*
YOU:	Will you remember me in an hour's time?
YOUR FRIEND:	*Yes.*
YOU:	Will you remember me in a minute's time?
YOUR FRIEND:	*Yes.*
YOU:	Will you remember me in a second's time?
YOUR FRIEND:	*Yes.*
YOU:	Knock knock.
YOUR FRIEND:	*Who's there?*
YOU:	You've forgotten me already.

14 LETTER BY LETTER

Look at this:

T 4.00 PM

What does it mean? Not a lot until you stop to think about it. It's the letter T followed by a time of day. That's it!

T 4.00 PM = TEA-TIME

How about this:

M A A W N A G Y E R

It's tricky. Written like this it should be a bit easier:

M a A w N a G y E R

I'll give you a clue. You are looking for the first four words of a famous Christmas carol. Now you see it, don't you?

M A A W N A G Y E R = AWAY in a MANGER

This next one is bit different. What have we here?

P O T O O O O O O O O

Any idea? Set out like this, you may find it easier:

P O T   O O O O O O O O

What is it? Pot and then eight Os – yes:

P O T O O O O O O O O = POTATOES

Now you've got the idea, have a go at this. You should get the first one in a flash. (And, yes, that *is* a clue.)

148   B O L T
     T H

149   M E
    A L

150   B E D

151   D N U O R

      G
152   G O
   N I

153   F E C D I S T A N T

154   T H E F L A S H P A N

155 O N C E
    N O O N

156 G B O

157 D
    L
    O
    H

158 P P P O D

159 O N E   A N O T H E R
    O N E   A N O T H E R
    O N E   A N O T H E R
    O N E   A N O T H E R
    O N E   A N O T H E R
    O N E   A N O T H E R

160 S Y M P H O N

161 E H C A

162 <u>S N O O Z E</u>
        U R

163 C A T N

164 C C C C C C

165 You might say this when you come
    home hungry, open the fridge and find
    nothing inside!
            O I C U R M T

15 ON THE MOVE

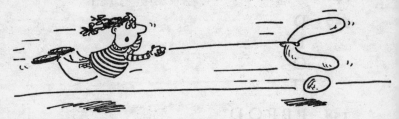

166 What goes out but never comes back?

167 What goes uphill and downhill but never moves?

168 What goes round the house and in the house and never touches the house?

169 What runs all day and all night and never stops?

170 What has a thousand legs and can't walk?

171 What is it goes from house to house and never goes in?

172 What goes round and round the wood and never gets into the wood?

173 What walks all day on its head?

174 What goes to the wood facing home?

175 What goes up and never comes down?

176 What is it that an aeroplane always travels with, cannot travel without, but is of no use to the aeroplane?

177 The more you take, the more you leave behind. What are they?

178 What goes up and down stairs without moving?

179 What has four wings and can't fly, no legs but can go?

180 What runs along the streets in London?

16 VERSE AND WORSE

Old riddles now, and all in rhyme,
Crack each one and take your time,
Feast yourself, have a guzzle
On six sweet nuts, each one a puzzle.

181   As round as an apple,
As deep as a pail;
It never cries out
Till it's caught by the tail.
What is it?

182   Formed long ago, yet made today,
Employed while others sleep;
What few would like to give away,
Nor many wish to keep.
What is it?

183   What force of strength cannot get
through,
I, with gentle touch, can do;
And many in the street would stand,
Were I not, as a friend, at hand.
What am I?

184 I washed my hands with water,
Which was neither rain nor run,
I dried them on a towel,
Which was neither woven nor spun.
How did I wash my hands?
How did I dry them?

185 Without a bridle,
Or a saddle,
Across a thing
I ride a-straddle,
And those I ride,
By help of me,
Though almost blind,
Are made to see.
What am I?

186 No mouth, no eyes,
Nor yet a nose,
Two arms, two feet,
And as it goes,
The feet don't touch the ground,
But all the way,
The head runs round.
What is it?

17 D-I-Y

Are you any good at do-it-yourself? Can you model with Plasticine or clay? Could you, for example, make a model of this?

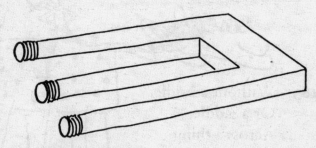

It's a trick question, because even if you think you could, you couldn't. There are some things than can be drawn, but can't be made.

Look at this box:

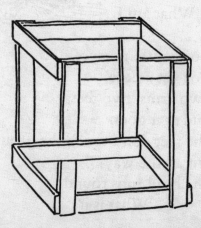

Believe it or not, even the cleverest carpenter in the world couldn't make it. It's a box you can design, but can't construct. Odd, isn't it?

From two impossible d-i-y challenges, let's turn to some others that are possible – just.

187   You have a ping-pong ball at the bottom of a hole in the ground. The hole is only a little wider than the ping-pong ball, but it's a lot deeper than your arm is. You can't do anything to extend your arm, so what can you do to get the ball out of the hole?

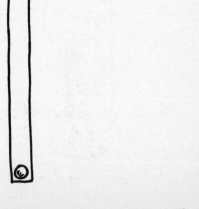

188 Take a five pound note and a 10p piece. Now try to balance the 10p on the edge of the five pound note.

Can it be done?

189 For this do-it-yourself riddle you need a large sheet of newspaper and two people. This is the question: How can two people stand on the same sheet of newspaper, face to face, so that they can neither see nor touch each other.

Their hands aren't tied, their eyes aren't closed and the sheet of newspaper must not be torn.

It can be done. Can you do it?

190   Tear up a piece of paper so that you have five small bits of paper. Now place the five bits of paper in the palm of your hand and blow them off *one by one.*

It can be done. Can you do it?

191   In 1492, Christopher Columbus didn't just sail the ocean blue, he also invented a most unusual riddle. This one: Can you take a hard-boiled egg and make it stand on its end without wobbling?

18 GOLDEN OLDIES

An English statesman called Charles James Fox, who was born in 1749 and died in 1806, enjoyed inventing riddles. This was one of his favourites:

'I went to the Crimea; I stopped there, and I never went there, and I came back again.

What am I?'

The answer is: *a watch*. It travelled with Fox to the Crimea. It stopped going when Fox was out there, never worked while he was there and Fox then brought it back to Britain.

The best riddles stand the test of time. See if you are foxed by these old favourites.

192   What do you lose every time you stand up?

193   Can you make a fire with only one stick?

194   What fastens two people yet touches only one?

195   It lives in winter,
Dies in summer,
And grows with its root upwards.
        What is it?

196   Light as a feather,
Nothing in it.
A stout man can't hold it
More than a minute.
        What is it?

197   If you feed it it will live,
If you give it water it will die.
        What is it?

198   I've seen you where you never were,
And where you ne'er will be;
And yet you in that very same place
May still be seen by me.
        What am I?

199 What goes up the chimney down,
But can't go down the chimney up?

200 Brass cap and wooden head,
Spits fire and spews lead.
    What is it?

201 Two legs sat upon three legs,
One leg knocked two legs off three legs,
Two legs hit four legs with three legs!
Can you work out what's going on?

202 What has a bed but never sleeps; and
has a mouth, yet never eats?

203 What is it which flies high and flies
low, has no feet and yet wears shoes?

204 At night they come without being fetched, and by day they are lost without being stolen.

>What are they?

205 As I went across the bridge, I met a man with a load of wood which was neither straight nor crooked.

>What kind of wood was it?

206 He who has it doesn't tell it;
He who takes it doesn't know it;
He who knows it doesn't want it.

>What is it?

207 What is filled every morning and emptied every night, except once a year when it is filled at night and emptied in the morning?

19 INTERNATIONAL ASSIGNMENT

From ancient riddles to modern ones, and five twentieth-century challenges that will take you east and west and even into outer space.

208 Fee Yat Uno is a Japanese school child who lives in the tallest block of flats in Tokyo. Every day he goes to school and gets the lift from his flat on the 39th floor to the ground. In the afternoons, when he comes home from school, he takes the lift to the 29th floor and walks up the remaining flights of stairs. Fee Yat Uno doesn't need the exercise, so why does he do it?

209 Michael Jackson was on a concert tour and staying at a large hotel in London. It was late at night and he had gone to bed, but he couldn't get to sleep. He sat up in bed, picked up the telephone on the bedside table and called the room next to his in the hotel. A voice answered.

'Is that Kylie Minogue?' asked Michael Jackson.

'No, of course not,' said the man who had answered the telephone.

Michael Jackson put his telephone down, smiled, and, thanks to the telephone call, went straight to sleep.

Can you explain Michael Jackson's behaviour?

210 Once upon a time, many moons ago, a Sultan had two sons. He also had a very great fortune. Instead of dividing his fortune between his two sons, the Sultan decided that he would give all of his fortune to the son whose horse lost a race in which the two sons had to compete together. Now both of the Sultan's sons were good horsemen. They knew how to win a race, but not how to lose one. Because naturally both of them wanted to gain their father's fortune, both were determined to lose the race, but they couldn't work out how to set about it.

What would you have advised them to do?

211 In the days of the old Wild West, a cowboy called Hank rolled into a ramshackle town in the heart of Texas. Hank had been out on the trail for more than a month and he needed a shave and a haircut. Hank quickly discovered that the town only had two barbers, each one with his own shop.

Hank looked inside the first shop where he saw the barber looking very smart, cleanly shaven and with his hair well-groomed and neatly cut.

Hank then looked into the second barber's shop. The place was in a dreadful mess and the barber himself was unshaven and had long, shaggy hair.

Hank gave the matter a little thought and then decided to use the second barber for his shave and haircut.

Why?

212   You are lost in space.

You have landed on an alien planet.

It could be Venus or it could be Mars.

All you know about Martians and Venusians is that Martians always tell the truth and Venusians always tell lies.

You need to know where you are, so you stop an alien passer-by.

You know the alien is either a Martian or a Venusian, but you don't know which.

You are allowed to ask the alien just one short question of not more than four words to find out where you are.

What is the question?

20 PICTURE RIDDLES

What's this?

A picture of two polar bears playing in a snow storm – of course!

What's this?

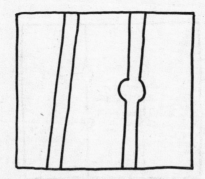

A picture of a stork with a wooden leg!

Now you've got the idea, have a go at these.

213   What's this?

214   What's this?

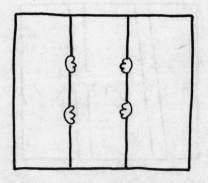

215 What's this?

216 What's this?

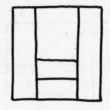

217 What's this?

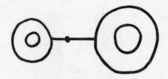

218 What's this?

219 What's this?

220 What's this?

221 What's this?

222 What's this?

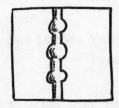

223 What's this?

224 Here's a horrid one to end with. What's this?

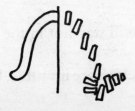

21 SILLY RIDDLES

Let's round off the riot of riddles with some riotously silly ones.

225   How many sweets can you put into an empty bag?

226   How can you leave a room with two legs and come back with six legs?

227   Why is snow different from Sunday?

228   What will stay hot in the refrigerator?

229   What letters are invisible, but never out of sight?

230 If your watch is broken, why can't you go fishing?

231 Why do you go to bed?

232 What do most gardeners not like to grow?

233 If a band plays in a thunderstorm, who is most likely to get hit by lightning?

234 What kind of band doesn't make music?

235 How could you fall off a twenty-foot ladder and not get hurt?

236 If you were to throw a white stone into the Red Sea, what would it become?

237 How can we tell that carrots are good for our eyes?

238 What's the difference between here and there?

239 Which Member of Parliament wears the largest hat?

240 Where do all people look exactly the same?

241 Captain Cook made three voyages round the world and was killed on one of them. Which one?

242 Why did the little girl put her head on the piano?

243   What kind of person always tries to make you smile?

244   Where and when can you never tell the truth?

245   Why did it take three Boy Scouts to take the old lady across the street?

246   Why do some people dress baby girls in pink and baby boys in blue?

247   I unwrapped a lump of sugar and put it in my coffee. The sugar didn't get wet. How come?

248   Why does a man's hair turn grey before his moustache?

249   I have a locked safe which contains two vases. All that is known about the vases is that one is gold and one is silver. Is there any way I can find out their colours without taking them out of the safe?

250   If frozen water is iced water, what is frozen ink?

ANSWERS

1   A map.
2   A glove.
3   The moon.
4   A broom.
5   A shoe.
6   Water.
7   Her baby before it's born.
8   A ship at anchor (the leaves are its sails).
9   A cherry.
10 A wedding ring.
11 A rope.
12 Hair.
13 A coffin.
14 Dove; olive leaf; Noah's ark.
15 An echo.
16 A needle and pin.
17 A towel.
18 A sieve.
19 It wasn't raining.
20 A sponge.
21 Hot water.
22 A river.
23 The Mississippi.
24 When the water is frozen into ice.
25 Rain.
26 They are in a funeral procession when it starts to rain. The man in the coffin stays dry, while the men carrying the coffin get wet.
27 He was bald.
28 A pencil.
29 A saw.

30   A mirror.

31   A candle (unlit and lit).

32   A bridge.

33   An egg.

34   A clock.

35   Coffee.

36   The postman.

37   They are husband and wife.

38   The boy's grandfather in the riddle is his mother's father,
     not his father's father.

39   No – he'd be dead.

40   Your mother.

41   His son.

42   Because there is not a single person in it.

43   Because he cannot be a brother and assist her too!

44   The surgeon, of course, was the mother of the injured child.

45   The height and width of the hat are exactly the same.

46   Both lines are the same length.

47   None.

48   They are both the same size.

49   It can be either – or both!

50   It can be inside or outside, depending on how it strikes you.

51   The garden fence.

52   Your name.

53   A hole.

54   A pack of cards.

55   An egg.

56   Tomorrow.

57   A cobweb.

58   A secret.

59   A lift attendant.

60   The window.

61   Nothing – it was a safety pin.

62   Mount Everest. It was still the highest, even if it hadn't
     been discovered.

63 The wind.
64 A saw.
65 A chair.
66 A railway track.
67 A bottle.
68 A clock.
69 A shoe.
70 The letter M.
71 Stockings.
72 A bed.
73 Your word.
74 'Are you asleep?'
75 Silence.
76 A mountain (it has mountaineers!).
77 An orange.
78 A vine.
79 A watermelon.
80 An egg.
81 Milk.
82 Corn on the cob.
83 A cabbage.
84 A cabbage.
85 An ear of corn.
86 From his ducks.
87 Lunch and dinner.
88 Three and a half minutes – if they're all boiled at the same time.
89 Envelope.
90 Post Office.
91 When you say 'I is the letter after H'.
92 In a dictionary.
93 The letter L.
94 Heroine (he, her, hero, heroine).
95 Alphabet.
96 The letter N.

97 School.

98 Peace.

99 Larry was a goldfish and Harry was a cat.

100 The lorry driver was walking.

101 White. It was a polar bear.

102 The short butcher is the daughter of the tall butcher.

103 The man was playing a game of Monopoly. His piece was a car and he landed on a property with a hotel on it. This meant that he had to give his money to the owner of the hotel.

104 It won't. The water will never cover the rung because as the water rises so does the ladder.

105. In 72 hours time it would be night again so there certainly would not be any sunshine.

106 The parrot was deaf.

107 A candle.

108 A squirrel.

109 A frog.

110 A tree.

111 A shoe.

112 Rain.

113 A clergyman.

114 Sunshine.

115 A potato.

116 Hair.

117 The letter R.

118 A sawmill.

119 Teeth.

120 One is taken up and shaken, the other is shaken up and taken.

121 One sells watches, the other watches cells.

122 One longs to eat, the other eats too long.

123 One is a mad bunny, the other is bad money.

124 One was made of wood, the other was Maid of Orleans.

125 Nothing – well, O is nothing!

126 One wears trousers, the other pants.

127 A dog can have fleas, but a flea can't have dogs.

128 Nothing. There is no such thing as a mummy bull.

129 A swallow.

130 A kitten.

131 A horse with a rider.

132 A bird in a cage.

133 A picture of an elephant.

134 A housefly.

135 A snake.

136 The rope wasn't tied to anything.

137 A spider's web.

138 A tadpole.

139 A horse.

140 Only the zebra. The others were coming away from it.

141 A cat.

142 A swallow.

143 Because they come in packs.

144 A snail.

145 A robin.

146 When they preen their feathers they get down in the mouth.

147 You think the answer is two, but it isn't. There won't be any birds left, because the shot will frighten the other two away.

148 Thunderbolt.

149 A square meal.

150 Bedspread.

151 Roundabout.

152 Going round in circles.

153 Disinfectant.

154 Flash in the pan.

155 Once upon a time.

156 Bingo.

157 Hold up.

158 Two peas in a pod.

159 Six of one and half a dozen of another.
160 Unfinished Symphony.
161 Backache.
162 You are under arrest.
163 Tin can.
164 The Seven Seas.
165 Oh, I see you are empty.
166 Your breath.
167 A road.
168 The sun.
169 A river.
170 500 pairs of trousers.
171 A path.
172 The bark of a tree.
173 A nail in a horseshoe.
174 An axe on a man's shoulder.
175 Smoke.
176 Noise.
177 Footsteps.
178 The carpet.
179 A windmill.
180 The kerb.
181 A bell.
182 A bed.
183 A key.
184 Washed in dew, dried in sunshine.
185 A pair of spectacles.
186 A wheelbarrow.
187 Pour water into the hole so that the ping-pong ball floats up to the surface.
188 Yes, but you have to fold the five pound note into a concertina shape before you can balance the coin on its edge.
189 To unravel the riddle you need a doorway. Place the sheet of newspaper so that half is one side of the door and half is on the other, with the door closed in between.

190 The way to do it is to use your fingers to hold four of the bits while you blow one off. You then hold three and blow another one off. Then you hold two, and so on.

191 This is how Christopher Columbus did it. He smashed the egg against the table, crushing the tip of the shell so that the egg would stand up on its own.

192 Your lap.

193 Yes, providing it's a matchstick.

194 A wedding ring.

195 An icicle.

196 Breath.

197 Fire.

198 Your reflection in a mirror.

199 An umbrella.

200 A gun.

201 A man sitting on a three-legged stool milking a cow is kicked by the cow, so the man hits the cow with the stool.

202 A river.

203 Dust.

204 Stars.

205 Sawdust.

206 Counterfeit money.

207 A stocking.

208 Fee Yat Uno isn't tall enough to reach higher than the button for the 29th floor!

209 The man in the next door bedroom was snoring very loudly. By telephoning him, Michael woke him up and stopped him snoring, which meant that Michael was able to get to sleep undisturbed.

210 The Sultan said that he would give all his fortune to the son whose horse lost the race, so you should advise each son to ride the other son's horse.

211 As there were only two barbers in the town, each must have cut the other one's hair. Hank chose the barber who had given his rival the cleaner shave and better haircut.

212 'Do you live here?' If you are on Mars, the answer will be 'Yes' because Martians always tell the truth and Venusians always lie. If you are on Venus, the answer will be 'No'.

213 A giraffe passing a first floor window.

214 A bear climbing a tree.

215 Two worms falling in love.

216 A dachshund passing a gap in a fence.

217 An aerial view of a Mexican frying an egg.

218 A spider performing the splits.

219 A mouse hiding behind a stone.

220 A black snake on a zebra crossing.

221 An aerial view of a Mexican walking along a railway line.

222 A spider performing a handstand.

223 A snake after swallowing three tennis balls.

224 A worm climbing over a razor blade.

225 Only one. After that it isn't empty.

226 When you come back, carry a chair with you.

227 Because it can fall on any day of the week.

228 Mustard.

229 The letters I and S.

230 Because you haven't the time.

231 Because the bed won't come to you.

232 Old.

233 The conductor.

234 A rubber band.

235 Fall off the bottom rung.

236 Wet.

237 Have you ever seen a rabbit wearing glasses?

238 The letter T.

239 The one with the largest head.

240 In the dark.

241 The last one.

242 She wanted to play by ear.

243 A photographer.

244 When you're lying in bed.

245 Because she didn't want to go.
246 Because they can't dress themselves.
247 When I unwrapped the lump of sugar, the coffee I put it
   into was a jar of instant coffee.
248 Because it's older.
249 Yes. One is gold and the other is silver.
250 Iced ink. (Don't worry – you don't really!)